The Curse of

27

The Curse of

27

Sarah Milne

A Pillar Box Red Publication

Contents

4 .... Introduction

7 .... Jim Morrison

17 .... Jimi Hendrix

27 .... Janis Joplin

37 .... Kurt Cobain

45 .... Brian Jones

55 .... Richey Edwards

61 .... Ron McKernan

65 .... Robert Johnston

71 .... Kristen Pfaff

75 .... Pete Ham

79 .... Pete De Freitas

81 .... Jean-Michel Basquiat

85 .... Amy Winehouse

93 .... The Others

Introduction

The Curse of 27, also known as The Forever 27 Club or just The 27 Club is not a club any of us would want to join. It is the name for a group of influential musicians from all over the world, representing all different genres of music, from all walks of life, all of whom have died at the age of just 27. And though their lives have been terribly short, these ill-fated artists have usually managed to cram more excitement and creative talent into their short lives than many of us will manage even if we live to be 100.

The members of The 27 Club certainly can lay claim to having made the most of their time on earth, and the motto 'Live Fast, Die Young' certainly applies to most of them. Living their life to the very fullest, working hard and partying even harder, the members have met their end in many different ways - poisoned, drowned, murdered, electrocuted, or just vanished into thin air. And though their deaths at such a young age are certainly a tragic waste, celebrating the work they left behind is a great way to remember the amazing talent that they displayed, and it's hard not to wonder how these talents would have matured over the years.

There are many myths and theories surrounding The Curse of 27. Some people think that looking into the world of numerology can explain why the number 27 seems to bring such bad luck, and some claim that more musicians die at this age than any other. It is said that Saturn appears in our zodiac charts between the ages of 27 and 30, and that this planet rules sorrow and regret, bringing huge change to our lives for those who are ready for it, and huge suffering for those who are not. Some people say that some of the members all had a white lighter on them at the time of death (though this is highly unlikely to be true). Whatever the reason behind The Curse of 27, whether you think there is some divine plan behind it, or it's just a case of bad coincidence, it certainly seems to be a crucial age for many of our greatest talents.

This book will take you through the most famous (or infamous) members of The 27 Club, from highly influential American blues singer Robert Johnson in the 1930s to British 'jazz singer' (as she liked to describe herself) Amy Winehouse in 2011, and chronicles their musical achievements, their ups and downs and of course, how they met with such an early death. We'll also run through some of the lesser-known members, some of them just as influential as the 'bigger' names we've all heard of. Whatever their talents, and however they are remembered, it's clear that each member of The 27 Club has left a permanent musical legacy behind, and are missed by family, friends and fans alike.

THE CURSE OF 27

Jim Morrison

Name: James Douglas Morrison

Born: December 8, 1943

Died: July 3, 1971

Cause of death: Heart failure, though no autopsy was performed

James Douglas Morrison was born in Florida, into a military family, the eldest of three siblings. His father George was in the US Navy (indeed later in his life he would reach the high rank of Rear Admiral), and this meant that the family moved around a lot when George was posted to different locations - in fact, all three Morrison siblings were born in different places. The Morrisons had both Irish and Scottish ancestors.

One of the most important events in young Jim's life is the story he told many times throughout his life, and one that was constantly referenced in his work, though the amount of truth in Jim's retellings has been disputed. The story goes something like this: Jim and his family were driving through the desert, when Jim witnessed a car crash on an American Indian reservation, with people crying, lying injured on the ground. Jim even said that he saw a dead body at the side of the road, but even his family are not sure about this. However much Jim may have exaggerated this story, the common consensus is that the Morrison family did see a car crash of some sort in the desert, young Jim did see an American Indian crying, and that this event left a permanent mark on his memory.

School Days

Jim was an avid reader at school, as well as throughout his life, especially drawn to the work of the German philosopher Friederich Nietzsche and the French poet Arthur Rimbaud. With a reported IQ of 149, Jim's keen intellect was often too much for his poor teachers, who often found him reading and referencing books they'd never even heard of. He was particularly interested in literature on existential philosophy, classic Greek and Latin works, as well as contemporary American authors such as Allen Ginsberg and Jack Kerouac.

Following high school, Jim moved to LA to study film at the University of California, Los Angeles (UCLA), completing his degree in 1965. After gaining his degree (in typical Jim style, he didn't attend his graduation ceremony) Jim became fully immersed in a bohemian way of life, living in Venice Beach, taking drugs (mostly LSD) and writing poetry that would later become some of The Doors early songs.

Opening The Doors

During this time Jim was reintroduced to Ray Manzarek, a fellow film student, and the two decided to form a band - a drummer and guitarist followed, and The Doors were born.

Taking their name from an Aldous Huxley book, 'The Doors of Perception', the band began writing songs, and performing in LA. In 1966, The Doors were the opening act for Irish singer Van Morrison at the infamous Whisky a Go Go club on Sunset Strip, and it is reported that Jim took a lot of influence from the way Van performed - becoming a brooding and sometimes menacing presence on stage.

After signing a record contract in 1967, The Doors' single 'Light My Fire' reached number one in the US

The Doors (l-r): Jim Morrison, John Densmore, Robby Krieger and Ray Manzarek.

charts. Following this success, the band appeared live on The Ed Sullivan Show, at the time one of America's most popular TV shows. Famously, the host had asked the band to change the lyric 'Girl we couldn't get much higher', replacing the word higher with better, as it was thought to be a reference to drug use. While the band assured Ed they would make this change, for one reason or another, they sang the original lyric, enraging Ed Sullivan who vowed never to have them on again.

Not that this ban mattered to The Doors - over the next few years they would release 4 albums and have a string of hits all over the world, reinforcing their success by performing to a global audience.

Under The Influence

Jim had always enjoyed himself to the fullest, and his interest in existentialism and the bohemian lifestyle meant that he often took mind-altering drugs to fuel the artistic process, but ultimately, his drug use and drinking had a negative effect on his creative thought processes. Following the release of The Doors fourth album, Jim would often show up to rehearsals and indeed live performances under the influence of either drink or drugs or both, and this led to the band performing without him. Once the very epitome of an attractive rock god, Jim also gained weight, grew a beard and gave up his famous tight leather trousers for slacks.

Au Revoir

In March 1971, Jim moved to Paris, where he seemed inspired by the city - often walking for hours through

JIM
MORRISON
POET
1943 - 1971

the old town, and he also shaved his beard and lost some weight. Jim's last studio recording was made at this time, accompanied by two American street musicians. He was found dead at his rented apartment in the city just a few months later on July 3. Longtime girlfriend Pamela Courson found him dead in the bath. The medical examiner at the time found no evidence of foul play, so, according to French law, no autopsy was performed.

Mythology

The lack of an official report into Jim's death has led to many myths and theories springing up regarding the circumstances of his demise. The official theory is that he died of heart failure, but how that failure came about is the topic of much debate. Some say it was brought on by a heroin overdose, some say he died of a brain hemorrhage. It is reported that in the few months leading up to his death, Jim had coughed up blood on a number of occasions, prompting some to think he was suffering from some form of respiratory disease.

Legend

Jim was buried in the Parisian cemetery Pere Lachaise, and the site remains one of the city's most visited tourist destinations - the grave is constantly covered in tributes to the man who christened himself 'The Lizard King'. Jim Morrison's legacy as a true rock and roll star lives on through the work of many musicians working today, and his work will continue to inspire for generations to come.

Jimi Hendrix

Name: Johnny Allen Hendrix / James Marshall Hendrix

Born: November 27, 1942

Died: September 18, 1970

Cause of death: Asphyxiation

Johnny Allen Hendrix was born on November 27, 1942 in Seattle Washington, the eldest of five siblings, and had Cherokee ancestry. His childhood was not a happy time. His father was sent to fight in World War II, and when he returned, he changed Johnny's name to James Marshall Hendrix, in memory of his late brother, Leon Marshall Hendrix. Struggling to find work, the family became very poor, and when he was just nine years old, Jimi's parents divorced. His mother, Lucille, died in 1958, following complications from cirrhosis of the liver, and at one point Jimi was sent to live with his paternal grandmother in Vancouver, Canada.

Learning To Play

Perhaps due to the disruption in his early life, Jimi was reported to be a shy and sensitive young man. He had already shown a liking for the guitar, and pretended to play it on a broomstick and an old ukulele, and when Jimi was around 15, he bought his first acoustic guitar for $5 from a friend of his father.

Jimi was delighted by his new instrument, and taught himself how to play by practicing for many hours a day, watching other guitar players and getting tips from them, and listening to records. Father Al then bought Jimi his first electric guitar in 1959, but he had no amplifier to use it with. Jimi started playing in local bands in and around Washington State, and it was during this time that Jimi picked up some of the outlandish stage behaviour he would become known for, such as playing the guitar behind his back or using his teeth to strum the strings.

In 1957 a young Jimi saw Elvis Presley perform in Seattle, and this led Jimi to have a particular fondness for the King. It was reported that Jimi had met Elvis during the time of this performance, but it's a fact that has been denied by Jimi's father Al.

Like many other teenage boys, Jimi found himself in trouble with the police - twice for being found in stolen cars. The punishment at that time was jail or the army, so Jimi chose the Army. He proved to be an unsuccessful soldier, and his commanding officers recommended he be discharged after a year, something Jimi didn't argue with. Though he made at least one lifelong friend during his time as a soldier, later in life Jimi talked of his dislike of the army itself.

Moving On

Following his time as a soldier, Jimi moved to Tennessee to make a living as a musician but grew bored of the scene in the south, so in January 1964, he moved to New York, where a month later, he won first prize in a talent contest at the Apollo Theatre. In March of the same year, Jimi's recording career started when he played as part of the Isley Brothers' band, then worked with legendary performer Little Richard.

A couple of years performing and recording with various artists followed, but Jimi's big break came when Linda Keith, the then girlfriend of Rolling Stones guitarist Keith Richards met Jimi, befriended him and

The Jimi Hendrix Experience (clockwise from top left): Mitch Mitchell, Noel. Redding and Jimi Hendrix.

recommended him to the Stones' producer, Andrew Loog Oldham. While Oldham didn't like Jimi's sound, another contact, Chas Chandler of The Animals, met Jimi and was impressed by his version of the song *Hey Joe*. They went back to London and a new band was formed, The Jimi Hendrix Experience.

Big Break

In 1966, following appearances on British TV shows Ready Steady Go, and Top of the Pops, word was getting out about Jimi's talent. His skill with the guitar and flair for performance meant he was becoming very well respected among his peer group - with guitar legends like Eric Clapton, Jeff Beck, Brian Jones, The Beatles and The Who becoming instant fans.

Jimi's version of *Hey Joe* was the first single to be released, followed by *Stone Free* and *Purple Haze*. All three were top ten hits in the UK.

Trans-Atlantic Success

Despite being an American, Jimi's success in the country of his birth only came about after Paul McCartney of The Beatles recommended the band to the organisers of a Californian music festival in 1967. This performance became legendary and was filmed, showing Jimi burn and smash up his guitar at the end of the set, something he would become notorious for.

Jimi's US success followed, and he met many of the most famous artists of the day, performing with some of the best talent of his generation, from Frank Zappa and BB King to Jim Morrison of the Doors. One of his most iconic performances came at the Woodstock Music Festival in 1969, where Jimi improvised a version of

Application Number PAS A 505221/1/97

CAUTION:—It is an offence to falsify a
certificate or to make or knowingly use a false
certificate or a copy of a false certificate
intending it to be accepted as genuine to the
prejudice of any person or to possess a
certificate knowing it to be false without
lawful authority.

QDX 171048

CERTIFIED COPY   OF AN ENTRY

DEATH	Entry No.	7

Registration district	Kensington	Administrative area
Sub-district	St. Mary Abbots	Royal Borough of Kensington and Chelsea

1. Date and place of death
Eighteenth September 1970
St. Mary Abbots Hospital. Kensington

2. Name and surname
Jimi HENDRIX otherwise
James Marshall HENDRIX

3. Sex Male

4. Maiden surname of woman who has married —

5. Date and place of birth
27th November 1942
United States of America

6. Occupation and usual address
a musician,
507/508 Cumberland Hotel
Great Cumberland Place, Marylebone.

7. (a) Name and surname of informant
Certificate received from G. Thurston. Coroner for Inner West
London. Inquest held 28th September 1970

(b) Qualification

(c) Usual address

8. Cause of death
Inhalation of vomit
Barbiturate intoxication (quinalbarbitone)
Insufficient evidence of circumstances
open verdict

9. I certify that the particulars given by me above are true to the best of my knowledge and belief .... Signature of Informant

10. Date of registration
Twentyninth September 1970.

11. Signature of registrar
E. M. Fisher   Registrar

CERTIFIED to be a true copy of an entry in the certified copy of a register of Deaths in the District above mentioned. Given at the GENERAL REGISTER OFFICE, under the Seal of the said Office on 8th October 1997

This certificate is issued in pursuance of the Births and Deaths Registration Act 1953. Section 34 provides that any certified copy of an entry purporting to be sealed or stamped with the seal of the General Register Office shall be received as evidence of the birth or death to which it relates without any further or other proof of the entry, and no certified copy purporting to have been given in the said Office shall be of any force or effect unless it is sealed or stamped as aforesaid.

the US national anthem, the *Star Spangled Banner* - now seen as a defining moment of the 1960s.

Throughout Jimi's life, he liked to take things to the extreme - he was a known womaniser, and had been involved with drink and drugs - he was reported to become violent when drunk, and was arrested for possession of drugs while going through customs at Toronto Airport in 1969.

Final Moments

Jimi's last performance was at Ronnie Scott's Jazz Club in London in 1970, where he performed with his latest band War. After that performance and a party Jimi was driven back to his girlfriend's flat in Notting Hill where sometime during the night he died. It was September 18, 1970. The official cause of death was asphyxiation, and doctors said he had suffocated on his own vomit. Some controversy still exists surrounding the circumstances and causes of Jimi's death.

Jimi was buried back in the US, but such was the level of interest in his grave that the remaining Hendrix family established a memorial site, away from the family burial plot. His tombstone features a Fender Stratocaster guitar. A fitting tribute to a flamboyant man who revolutionised the way guitars are played to this day.

THE CURSE OF 27

Friends of the late rock star Jimi Hendrix carry his coffin from the church after funeral services, 1 October, 1970 in Seattle. Pallbearers include Herbert Price, left, Hendrix' valet; Donny Howell behind Price; and Eddie Rye, front right.

Janis Joplin

Name: Janis Lyn Joplin

Born: January 19, 1943

Died: October 4, 1970

Cause of death: Heroin overdose

Janis Lyn Joplin was born and raised in Texas, the eldest of three siblings. Her parents recalled that the young Janis was always a bit more needy than her brother and sister, and needed a lot of attention to keep her happy. The family attended church regularly and Janis began her performing career by singing in the local church choir.

Teenage years are notoriously hard for many people, but for Janis they seemed to be particularly troubled times. She was overweight and had deep acne scars, so as well as looking different to the other children, she also liked different things - reading, painting, blues and folk music. Many of her friends were African Americans, in a time of continuing racial prejudice. Janis once said that she was effectively shunned in high school. Later, when she was asked whether she had been popular at school, Janis laughed and said that her classmates had:

"laughed me out of class, out of town and out of the state".

Somewhat surprisingly she attended a 10 year reunion for her classmates, but it wasn't a happy event for her.

Early Days

After graduating from High School, Janis went to a local college, but did not complete her studies - perhaps she was unhappy, perhaps she knew she was destined for bigger and better things. After recording her first song, *What Good Can Drinkin Do*, at a friend's house in December 1962, she left Texas for San Francisco in early 1963, and headed for the hippy hot spot of Haight Ashbury.

The following year, she recorded some blues songs, accompanied by a typewriter as a percussion instrument, and it was round about this time of year that her once-occasional drug use escalated to become heavy. Janis was a regular drinker, and was known to take a lot of amphetamine, becoming known as a speed freak, and started dabbling in heroin - the drug that would eventually kill her.

New Start

The drugs had started to take their toll, and Janis's friends managed to persuade her to head back to Texas in 1965. While there, Janis managed to change her lifestyle, avoiding alcohol and drugs, going back to university and leading a sober life. During this time, she continued to perform on stage, singing her own songs and playing guitar.

Despite this 'new start' Janis eventually went back to San Francisco in 1966, as she had been asked to join psychedelic rock band Big Brother and the Holding Company - her amazing blues-influenced voice had attracted the attention of the band who wanted her to join them on stage. Janis managed to avoid drugs until 1966, when the band moved in with legendary group The Grateful Dead. Janis and the band started to become successful, appearing on American TV in 1968, when the group were referred to as Janis Joplin

and Big Brother and the Holding Company. This shift of focus from the band as a whole to Janis as a front woman caused tensions among the other members of the band, who thought Janis was becoming too much of an ego. Janis left the band at the end of 1968.

Change Of Scene

Janis then formed a new band, the Kozmic Blues Band, and while they were successful, Janis by this time was addicted to heroin, reportedly using up to $200 worth of the drug per day.

The next few years were spent touring and performing, with another band, the Full Tilt Boogie Band, and Janis even managed another period free of drink and drugs in Brazil in 1970.

Backward Step

Back in Los Angeles, later that year, Janis's drug use had again resurfaced and she was also drinking heavily. She was rehearsing for and recording her latest studio album, and was in a steady relationship with 21 year old student, Seth Morgan. One of the last things she recorded was a happy birthday greeting to John Lennon, a present that he received after her death.

Janis's Death

On Sunday October 4, 1970, Janis failed to appear at the recording studios, and her producer became worried, heading to the hotel she was staying in. He saw Janis's brightly coloured Porsche in the car park and when he got to her room, found Janis dead. The official cause of death was a heroin overdose, and it's widely accepted that Janis died because the heroin

she used that night was much stronger than she was used to.

After a private funeral, attended only by Janis's parents and aunt, Janis's ashes were scattered from a plane into the Pacific Ocean. Her Will however, had left money to throw a party after her death, and this happened at the end of October 1970, in San Francisco. Perhaps befitting for a hippy send off, hash brownies were given out during the party.

Though her death was certainly shocking to her friends and to her fans (especially as it came only 16 days after Jimi Hendrix had been found dead), Janis's legacy has been extremely important, especially for female performers. She truly was a pioneer for women in a time when the music world was a massively male dominated place. Many female artists that followed, from Stevie Nicks of Fleetwood Mac to Florence Welch from Florence and the Machine have stated that Janis was a huge influence on their aspirations to be performers, as well as their musical tastes.

Lasting Legacy

More than just a singer, a songwriter, a performer, Janis was in every sense an artist - inexplicably linked to her work, which could be both gut wrenchingly painful and gorgeously beautiful. She gave everything to her work, managing to turn the agony of an unhappy childhood and painful relationship breakdowns into the most amazing songs and mesmerising performances, but in the end, her addictions got the better of her. Janis Joplin was a true one-off free spirit and (apart from the drug use), an inspiration to women artists everywhere.

THE CURSE OF 27

Kurt Cobain

Name: Kurt Donald Cobain

Born: February 20, 1967

Died: April 5, 1994

Cause of death: Suicide

Kurt Donald Cobain, was born in 1967, in Aberdeen, in the US state of Washington, with younger sister Kimberley arriving three years later. His family was a musical and artistic one, and many of Kurt's relations played in bands or were artists. The young Kurt was said to be sensitive and caring as well as extremely creative - his bedroom was filled with (extremely accurate) drawings of his favourite cartoon characters, so much so that it looked like an art studio. His aunt recalls Kurt starting to sing at the age of two. At four, he had started playing the piano and making up his own songs, as well as singing along with some contemporary hits.

Early Days

Kurt's happy childhood was dealt a shattering blow, when his parents divorced - he was just eight years old. This event is one which is said to have had a profound effect on Kurt's demeanour at the time, and for the rest of his life. The previously happy and excitable little boy became defiant and withdrawn, and his state of mind wasn't helped by his parent's separately becoming involved with new partners. In fact, Kurt's behaviour became so bad that therapists recommended his parents get back together to provide him with a stable home. This didn't happen and Kurt's father was given full custody of Kurt, but even family life couldn't tame Kurt's teenage rebellion, and his father sent him off to live with various families and friends over the years.

High school continued to be a difficult time for Kurt, who preferred to spend his time drawing pictures, writing in his diary, listening to music and reading the religious teachings of Jainism and Buddhism. His love of punk rock grew, and his first concert, to see The Melvins (sometimes known as the godfathers of grunge) had a big effect on Kurt.

Nirvana

After dropping out of high school, Kurt was kicked out of home and moved into an apartment, paying the rent by working at a holiday resort. In 1987, Kurt formed Nirvana with bassist Krist Novoselic, who he had been at high school with (Dave Grohl would follow as drummer in 1990). The band quickly established itself on the Seattle grunge scene, and their first album, *Bleach*, was released in 1989. But it was *Smells Like Teen Spirit* , the first single from their second album *Nevermind* which was a (surprise) worldwide hit, catapulting the band from a small corner of the Northwest Pacific to global success.

Nevermind is now seen as one of the most important albums of the nineties, and certainly one of the defining moments of the grunge scene. Its popularity paved the way for many other Seattle based grunge bands, such as Pearl Jam, Alice in Chains and Soundgarden, and the subculture of grunge was to become mainstream - a victim of its own success.

Reluctant Hero

Kurt, it seems, was never comfortable being in the spotlight, and while other artists seem to thrive on the attention of the audience, he was petrified about

going on stage, and started to self-medicate using drugs such as valium and heroin to numb his fear. Of course, it didn't help when the media pigeonholed him as the voice of a generation, holding him up to be the unofficial spokesperson for the grunge movement - Kurt hated this side of things.

Kurt's drug use escalated, getting so bad that in 1990, he kept falling asleep during a photo shoot, and in 1993, just before Nirvana were due to go onstage in New York, he suffered a heroin overdose. Wife Courtney Love didn't call an ambulance, instead injecting him with an antidote. Kurt went onstage and performed to an audience none the wiser.

Beginning Of The End

A troubled state of mind led to Kurt's first suicide attempt in March 1994, where he overdosed on a combination of champagne and Rohypnol while in

Rome with Courtney. This time he was released from hospital after five days. Later that month, back in Seattle, the police were called to Kurt and Courtney's home, and confiscated several guns and bottles of pills from the property.

By this time, Kurt's friends and family were gravely concerned for his health, both mental and physical, and an intervention was arranged, where his closest friends sat him down and persuaded him to try to kick his addictions. By the end of this session, Kurt had agreed to go to a detox centre and start his rehabilitation. The next day, however, he escaped from the centre in LA and headed back to his home in Seattle.

Kurt was found dead at his home on April 8, 1994, by a workman who had arrived at the house to install a security system. The workman at first thought Kurt was simply sleeping, but then noticed a little blood coming from his ear and a shotgun pointing at his chin. Kurt had committed suicide and left a long note to his wife and child (Frances Bean Cobain was one year and eight months at the time of her father's death). The coroner estimated his date of death to be April 5.

Music fans everywhere were devastated to hear of Kurt's death, and at a public vigil held two days after the body was found, 7000 mourners turned up to show their respects.

The Legend Lives On

Despite such a troubled end, Kurt's work lives on today, and he left behind him a musical and artistic legacy that continues to inspire young musicians today. Just as Kurt himself was inspired by bands like The Pixies, The Stooges and The Velvet Underground, Nirvana

inspires the next generation - indeed, in 2006, Kurt became the top earning deceased celebrity - testament to the importance of his catalogue of work.

Kurt Cobain was quite simply one of the most important and influential musicians of his time, leaving behind some of the greatest songs of the late 20th century. We were lucky to have had him, even for such a short while.

Nirvana (l-r): Dave Grohl, Chris Novoselic, Kurt Cobain and Pat Smear

Brian Jones

Name: Lewis Brian Hopkins Jones

Born: February 28, 1942

Died: July 3, 1969

Cause of death: Death by misadventure

Brian Jones was born in Cheltenham on February 28, 1942, into a middle class family, and had two younger sisters. Brian's parents were very musical - his mother Louisa was a piano teacher and father Lewis played piano and organ as well as leading the choir in the local church. Perhaps the family's Welsh origins meant that a love of music was in their blood.

The first 'modern' music that Brian felt an affinity with was the work of American jazz saxophonist Cannonball Adderley, which Brian first heard in 1957. This led to Brian's interest in jazz and he managed to persuade his parents to buy him a saxophone, which he cherished. An acoustic guitar followed two years later, a present for his 17th birthday.

School Life

At school Brian certainly had the brains required to be a model pupil - finally getting 9 O-levels and 2 A-levels, but a rebellious streak led to a hostility toward figures of authority. Even at a young age, Brian hated conforming to rules, disliked his uniform and frequently talked back to the teachers, and this no doubt led to his suspension from school on a number of occasions.

Brian's eye for the ladies also started at a fairly young age when his 14 year old girlfriend fell pregnant (he was just 17 himself). In the 1950s teenage pregnancies

The Rolling Stones (l-r): Mick Jagger, Bill Wyman, Brian Jones, Keith Richards and Charlie Watts.

were a completely different matter than they are today and the gravity of the situation led Brian to quit his school in disgrace. His girlfriend had a boy but gave him up for adoption.

After quitting school, Brian took himself off to Europe to travel and work for a summer, pleased to get away from the scandal of the unplanned pregnancy. He travelled through northern Europe and Scandinavia, busking and leading the free life of a wandering minstrel, though his tales of this time in his life were often said to be exaggerated for effect.

Starting Out

On his return to Britain, Brian started playing at small jazz and blues clubs, which along with odd jobs and busking, kept him afloat. His wandering eye meant that babies followed in 1959, 1963, 1964, 1965 and 1969 all to different women.

After leaving Cheltenham for London, in 1962 Brian put an advert in a local music paper inviting musicians to audition for a new R&B band. Pianist Ian Stewart and singer Mick Jagger applied, with Jagger bringing along his childhood friend Keith Richards to rehearsals. The first incarnation of The Rolling Stones was born, and the band played their first gig at London's infamous Marquee Club in May 1962. Additional members of the line-up included Bill Wyman on bass guitar and Charlie Watts on drums, and the band was complete. At this stage, Brian was still very much at the forefront of organising the band and driving them forward - in fact he was the band's business manager for a while, earning £5 more per week than the other members of the band. This inequality would lead to tensions

The Rolling Stones (l-r): Brian Jones, Mick Jagger,
Charlie Watts, Keith Richards and Bill Wyman.

between Brian and the other members of the band.

Over the next few years, The Rolling Stones became one of the UK's biggest bands, and Brian was still making a huge contribution to their success. In particular Brian and Keith Richards worked on playing their guitars in such a way that it was extremely hard to tell which was lead and which was rhythm, and in fact this sound became a hallmark of any Stones record. Brian still played harmonica and sometimes performed backing vocals on the recordings.

With great success came a shift in the focus for the band - producer Andrew Loog Oldham arrived to work with the Stones, and Brian's place as top dog was slowly usurped by Mick Jagger and Keith Richards. Tensions arose, not only from this but from constant touring and eventually Brian's drug use and heavy drinking.

The Beginning Of The End

Brian began to rely more and more on drugs and alcohol as a coping mechanism, leading to his alienation from the band, and of course, a huge drop in his musical contributions. His last appearance with the band was in 1968. The following year, when The Rolling Stones were about to set off to America for a tour, Brian was told by the other members that he was out of the band he had formed - his previous drug convictions meant that he would not get a work visa to go to the US.

After leaving the Stones, Brian retreated to his country estate in East Sussex and conflicting reports say that at this time he was both mentally unstable, and the happiest he'd ever been. Whatever state of mind Brian was in at the time, didn't help him on July 3, 1969, when he was found at the bottom of his swimming pool at his house. While his girlfriend was convinced he had a pulse when he was taken out of the pool, Brian was pronounced dead at the scene, his heart and liver enlarged by heavy drug and alcohol use.

Unexplained?

The cause of death on the coroner's report was 'death by misadventure', commonly thought of as drowning. Over the years, however, there have been many different theories about what happened to Brian in

The Rolling Stones (l-r): Brian Jones, Mick Jagger,
Charlie Watts, Keith Richards and Bill Wyman

his final moments - indeed, one rumour is that he was murdered by a builder working on his house, and it has been reported that many things, including furniture and recordings, were stolen from the house after Brian's death.

Two days after Brian's death, The Rolling Stones performed at the legendary free Hyde Park Concert, dedicating the concert to Brian. Hundreds of white butterflies were released in tribute to Brian. The Who, Jimi Hendrix and Jim Morrison of The Doors all paid public tribute to the founder member of the Stones, and Brian was buried in a coffin sent as a present from Bob Dylan. A fitting end for the founding member of one of the UK's most influential and long lasting bands.

THE CURSE OF 27

Richey Edwards

Name: Richard James Edwards

Born: 22 December, 1967

Disappeared: 1 February, 1995

Missing presumed dead since 2008

Richard James Edwards was born on December 22, 1967 and grew up in Blackwood, South Wales. After school, he studied at the University of Wales in Swansea, where he graduated with a 2:1 degree in political history.

Early Days

Richey Edwards (or Richey James as he was sometimes known during his time in the Manic Street Preachers) was first a driver and roadie for the band, who had all attended the same school, but soon was accepted as the fourth member, which already consisted of cousins Sean Moore, James Dean Bradfield and friend Nicky Wire - despite the fact that he had little or no ability for playing guitar or singing.

This apparent lack of musical talent seemed to cause no barrier for Richey, who more often than not found himself to be the band's spokesman. He may have mimed playing the guitar at some of the band's early live gigs, but along with Nicky his contribution to the band's lyrics was essential.

Commitment

Richey became infamous in the British music press in 1991 when journalist Steve Lamaq interviewed the band for the NME following a gig in Norwich. Steve had questioned the authenticity of the Manics' punk ethos, and asked Richey how serious he was about his art. Richey's response was to carve the words '4Real' into his forearm using a razorblade he happened to be carrying. Richey's arm needed 18 stitches, the Manics made headline news, and Steve Lamaq was in no doubt about their commitment to the cause.

Richey's lyrical genius was often tinged with heartbreaking sadness, and he was open about the bouts of severe depression he suffered from throughout his life. The band's third album, *The Holy Bible*, is one of their darker works, and one which Richey is said to have written 80% of. The mood of the album seemed to reflect his state of mind, and following its release, Richey checked into The Priory.

Final Appearance

Following his time at The Priory, Richey rejoined the band, touring Europe in 1994. He appeared on stage with the Manics for the last time at the London Astoria on December 21, 1994, when the gig ended with the band smashing up all their equipment.

The Manic Street Preachers were due to fly out to America on February 1, 1995 for a promotional tour, but Richey had disappeared. He had consistently withdrawn money from his bank account in the two weeks leading up to his disappearance. On the day in question, he checked out of his London hotel at 7am, and drove to his home in Cardiff. Various sightings were reported in the two weeks that followed, and his car was given a ticket on February 14 at a service station, close to the Severn Bridge, a notorious suicide spot. It was classed as abandoned three days later and reported that it had been lived in.

Final Mystery

Despite subsequent sightings of Richey in Goa and the Canary Islands, he was presumed dead in 2008. The ninth album by the Manic Street Preachers, *Journal for Plague Lovers*, released in 2009, entirely consisted of lyrics left behind by Richey. We may not ever know for sure what happened to Richey Edwards, but we can still enjoy his beautiful, heart-rending lyrics.

Ron McKernan

Name: Ronald Charles McKernan

Born: September 8, 1945

Died: March 8, 1973

Cause of death: Gastrointestinal hemorrhage associated with alcoholism

Ron 'Pigpen' McKernan, along with the legendary Jerry Garcia, founded one of the most important bands of the late 60s / early 70s. Ron was born in San Bruno, California, where his father was an R&B and blues DJ. His father's love of blues no doubt rubbed off on young Ron, who taught himself how to play blues guitar at an early age.

Alcohol Abuse

Ron began drinking whilst very young, and following his early departure from high school, he started hanging round record shops and coffee houses, and it was here that he met Jerry Garcia, who by that time was already performing. Jerry asked Ron to accompany him on stage one night, and Ron and Jerry jammed together on a regular basis.

The Grateful Dead

In The Grateful Dead, which formed around 1965, Ron played the blues organ and harmonica as well as providing vocals for the band. He was given the nickname 'Pigpen' because his band mates thought he looked very similar to the character of the same name from the cartoon strip Peanuts.

The Grateful Dead were well known for being a band to take most things to extremes, but while his band mates were experimenting with psychedelic drugs such as LSD, Ron stuck to alcohol, consuming large quantities of Southern Comfort and Thunderbird wine.

In the early 70s, The Grateful Dead had become more and more popular, and found themselves touring the world. Ron had a short relationship with another victim of The Curse of 27, Janis Joplin, and worryingly started to display symptoms of cirrhosis of the liver, even at this young age. He was admitted to hospital in 1971, where a doctor told him that he should not tour again, but Ron found that he was bored without a life on the road, and so went back on the road again.

Ill Health

While touring made him happy, it did not agree with his health, and he made his last appearance with The Grateful Dead at the Hollywood Bowl in June 1972.

Ron was found dead at home in California on March 8, 1973. He had died of a gastrointestinal hemorrhage, brought on by the effects of alcoholism. He is buried in Palo Alto.

Ron's legacy lives on through the continuing popularity of The Grateful Dead. While they may not be to everyone's musical tastes, they certainly changed the way we expect a band to behave and evolve.

THE CURSE OF 27

Robert Johnson

Name: Robert Leroy Johnson

Born: May 8, 1911

Died: August 16, 1938

Cause of Death: Reported to be strychnine poisoning

Robert Leroy Johnson was born in Mississippi, in America's Deep South in 1911. His childhood was a harder life than most of us have today, growing up in a time of great poverty and prejudice, and he was sent to live with his stepfather in Memphis for some years, only rejoining his mother in Mississippi when he was around seven or eight years old. He was known by the name of Robert Spencer when he was growing up, but by the time of his marriage in 1929, he had become Robert Johnson and so signed his name, after the name of his biological father.

Early Tragedy

Robert's marriage, at the tender age of just 17, to Virginia Travis was cut tragically short, when his new wife died the following year in childbirth. As it would be for anyone, this event was a turning point in Robert's life, having a huge effect on his plans for the future. Some of Virginia's relatives believed that her death was Robert's punishment for singing songs out of church - and that by performing these secular songs, he was selling his soul to the devil. Whatever the case, Virginia's death was the catalyst for Robert's change of direction, and he gave up any dreams of a settled family life, instead preferring to become a fulltime blues musician. He never lived a settled life again, instead travelling all over America playing in blues clubs and on street corners, staying with relatives, or musical peers, and forming relationships with many different women.

Schoolfriends have said that Robert was already an accomplished player of the harmonica and jaw harp (said to be one the oldest musical instruments in the world), but it seems that his ability to play blues guitar was a skill that took him longer to acquire, one that he learned from well-respected blues musicians of the day.

Guitar Hero

His guitar playing became so good so quickly, that it was said that Robert had made a pact with the devil - a legend that had its roots in the classic German legend of Faust who made a deal with the devil, giving him his soul in return for unlimited knowledge, and one that is revisited in the 1980s movie Crossroads. At the time, many of the greatest guitar players were reported to have heightened their talents by drawing energy from playing guitar in graveyards at night.

Whatever the reason for Robert's talent, it was one he quickly became well-respected for, and his style of playing is said to have introduced Delta Blues and the slide guitar to a much wider audience.

The musical industry was of course, very different than than it is now, and during his lifetime, Robert only stepped into a recording studio a few times - for three days in 1936, where he played 16 songs, and twice in the following year. Eleven of his records were released while he was alive.

Severe Pain

A womaniser and drinker, Robert could often be found playing the night away at a rural jook joint. In August 1938, he had been playing for a few weeks at a country jook near Greenwood Mississippi. Despite the various theories that have been bandied about for years, the now widely accepted story goes that Robert had been carrying on an affair with the jook joint manager's wife, whose husband had provided her with a drink laced with the poison strychnine to give to Robert. He took ill not long afterward, but it took at least two to three, maybe as many as six weeks for him to succumb, and he died in severe pain. The date of his death, August 16, 1938 has been known for over 40 years, though his final resting place has only relatively recently been confirmed by eye witness testimony in the year 2000. Despite the existence of 3 tombstones - all in Leflore County, Mississippi, only the one at Little Zion Church, north of Greenwood, is bona fide.

Post Mortem Fame

Following his death, Robert's work still remained known only to a small percentage of music fans, indeed it is said that 20 years after his death hardly anyone knew his name or his work. It is widely accepted that it was Robert's rediscovery by white (mostly British) musicians in the 1960s that led to a revival of his work and his establishment as an innovator and blues legend.

THE CURSE OF 27

Musical Influence

Among his most famous fans is Keith Richards of The Rolling Stones. Ironically it was Keith's ex-bandmate, and fellow member of the 27 Club, Brian Jones, that introduced Keith to Robert's work, and he was a massive influence on Keith's guitar playing, still remaining one of his biggest influences: "Robert Johnson's the apex of blues songwriting, guitar-playing and singing". The Rolling Stones performed or recorded 3 of Robert's songs - *Kind Hearted Woman Blues, Love In Vain Blues* and *Stop Breakin' Down Blues*.

Robert Plant of Led Zeppelin is also someone who cited Robert as an influence on his style, referring to him as "Robert Johnson, to whom we all owed our existence, in some way". The band recorded *Traveling Riverside Blues*, based on Robert's original song.

Eric Clapton, himself a legendary guitar player, has called Robert "the most important blues musician who ever lived", and his album *Me and Mr Johnson* was a tribute to Robert's work.

It's clear that Robert Johnson has become more famous and renowned in death than he could ever have hoped to in his lifetime. No doubt he would have been happy inspiring future generations of music lovers, and his work is certain to continue influencing generations to come.

THE CURSE OF 27

(l-r): Drummer Patty Schemel, singer Courtney Love and bassist Kristen Pfaff of American rock group Hole.

Kristen Pfaff

Name: **Kristen Marie Pfaff**

Born: **May 26, 1967**

Died: **June 16, 1994**

Cause of death: **Heroin overdose**

Kristen Marie Pfaff was born in Buffalo, New York, on May 26, 1967. After school and a period living in Europe, Kristen attended Boston College and then the University of Minnesota, where she studied classical piano and cello. After graduation and while still living in Minneapolis, Kristen taught herself how to play bass guitar, and formed her first band, Janitor Joe.

Janitor Joe

As well as Kristin on bass guitar, Janitor Joe consisted of guitarist/vocalist Joachim Breuer and drummer Matt Entsminger. They released their first single, *Hmong* in 1992, and followed this up with three more singles and an album, *Big Metal Birds*. The band were becoming well known on the grunge circuit that was forming in and around Minneapolis, with Kristen's relentless style of playing bass being an integral part of Janitor Joe's sound. In 1993 Janitor Joe toured the US.

Moving On

During the Californian leg of their US tour, Kristen was noticed by Eric Erlandson and Courtney Love of Hole, who at that time were looking for a new bassist. Courtney invited Kristen to come and play with them, but she said no. Never one to be defeated, Courtney kept trying to lure Kristen to Hole, and it is reported that Kristen's father persuaded her this was a decision that made commercial sense - moving from a relatively small, albeit successful band, to one that had a worldwide presence.

In 1993, Kristen moved from Minneapolis to Seattle to join Hole and work on their second album, *Live Through This*. She worked closely with Eric, Courtney and Courtney's husband Kurt Cobain, and started a relationship with Eric, which lasted most of that year.

Dependency

While Kristen had been known to experiment with drugs in Minneapolis, Seattle was at that time known as the heroin capital of America, and she gradually got into heavier drug use. Rehab at the end of 1993 followed, and in early 1994 Kristen took herself away from Hole and Seattle to tour with Janitor Joe once more. Just after her return to Seattle, her friend Kurt Cobain committed suicide, and Kristen decided to go back to Minneapolis to rejoin Janitor Joe permanently.

Final Moment

On June 16, 1994, the day Kristen was planning to move home to Minneapolis, she was found dead in her apartment. Her death was ruled accidental and put down to acute opiate intoxication.

Kristen was buried in her home town of Buffalo, and a scholarship in her name was set up at the University of Minnesota, to be awarded to individuals active in the arts in the pursuit of their educational goals. A fitting tribute to a great musician.

Badfinger (l-r): Tom Evans, Pete Ham and Mike Gibbins

Pete Ham

Name: Peter William Ham

Born: April 27, 1947

Died: April 24, 1975

Cause of death: Suicide

Pete Ham is best known as the leader of the rock band Badfinger, who were signed to The Beatles' record label, Apple in the 1960s.

Born in Swansea, Wales, Pete formed his first band in 1961, The Panthers, and the band then evolved into The Iveys. After moving to London (the centre of the British music scene), they were heard by Ray Davies of The Kinks, who was impressed by them and even produced a few of their tracks. It was Mal Evans, however, that ensured the band got the break they deserved. Mal worked as The Beatles' personal assistant, who again was so impressed by the band that he played some tracks to all four Beatles, and they were in agreement - this band should be signed to Apple, their recently launched record label.

Early Days

After being signed, the band changed their name to Badfinger, and their debut release, *Come and Get It* (co-written by Paul McCartney) became a top ten hit all over the world. Badfinger then followed this success with two more hits, *No Matter What* and *Baby Blue*.

For Pete himself, a career in songwriting was becoming more and more likely. He co-wrote the song *Without You,* made famous by Harry Nilsson in 1972 and covered many times since - it's well known as one of Mariah Carey's signature songs too. The composition received critical acclaim as well as commercial success, and it won the highly prestigious Ivor Novello Award for Song of the Year in 1973.

By then, The Beatles' record label was in deep trouble, so Badfinger signed to Warner Brothers, but this change in management brought trouble for the band. Legal wrangles and financial troubles proved to have a negative influence on the band's creativity.

The Decline

In 1975, the band were effectively not working anymore, meaning Pete and the rest of the members were left with no income, while still tied to Warner Brothers. This had a big effect on Pete's state of mind, and he was found hanged in the garage of his home that same year.

One can only guess the agony that Pete was feeling at the time - he was reported to be suffering signs of mental distress in the months running up to his death - he left behind a girlfriend pregnant with his daughter (born one month later), and an angry suicide note which had no kind words to say about the band's business manager.

Pete's life may have ended in unhappiness, but he did leave a legacy behind. He is widely credited as being one of the inventors of power pop. Whenever you next hear Mariah belting out *Without You*, spare a thought for Pete Ham, the songwriter from Swansea.

Badfinger (l-r): Pete Ham, Joey Molland,
Mike Gibbons and Tommy Evans.

Badfinger (l-r): Pete Ham, Tommy Evans, Mike Gibbons and Joey Molland.

Echo and the Bunnymen (l-r): Ian McCulloch, Pete de Freitas, Will Sergeant and Les Pattinson.

Pete De Freitas

Name: Pete Louis Vincent de Freitas

Born: August 2, 1961

Died: June 14, 1989

Cause of death: Motorcycle accident

Pete Louis Vincent de Freitas was born in Port of Spain, the capital of Trinidad and Tobago in 1961, and went to school in Somerset.

Echo And The Bunnymen

He joined Echo & the Bunnymen in 1980, replacing the band's drum machine. Their debut album, *Crocodiles*, received much critical acclaim in the music press, and became a top 20 hit in the UK charts

Over the next few years and until the band split in 1988, Echo and the Bunnymen released many hit singles, including *Bring on the Dancing Horses*, *The Killing Moon* and *Seven Seas*. Their work was often featured on film soundtracks, with their cover version of The Doors' *People Are Strange* being one of the standout tracks on The Lost Boys soundtrack.

Pete's skill as a drummer was well known and has been favourably compared to Foo Fighters frontman Dave Grohl, who has a reputation of being one of the most impressive drummers of his generation.

Fatal Accident

Pete died in a motorcycle accident two months before his 28th birthday riding from London to Liverpool. He was riding his Ducati on the A51 near Stafford when someone pulled out in front of him.

Andy Warhol (left) and Jean-Michel Basquiat.

Jean-Michel Basquiat

Name: Jean-Michel Basquiat

Born: December 22, 1960

Died: August 12, 1988

Cause of Death: Heroin overdose

Jean-Michel Basquiat was an extremely talented artist, poet and performer. The son of a Haitian father and Puerto Rican mother, Jean-Michel was introduced to many cultural references at a young age, and his intelligence shone through, even as a child in New York - he could read and write at the age of four, and was fluent in three languages at the age of 11.

His career in art began as a teenager, when he and a couple of his friends started spray painting graffiti on buildings in the Manhattan area of the city. He was subsequently involved in many artistic movements in New York, from starting a noise rock band called Gray, to starring in indie films, and even music videos - he can be seen in the video for Blondie's disco inspired hit *Rapture* as a DJ in a nightclub.

Artistic Scene

Jean-Michel was at the heart of New York's artistic scene in the 1980s - in fact, as well as briefly dating Madonna in 1982, the same year he worked with megastar David Bowie. In 1980, Jean-Michel was introduced to seminal artist Andy Warhol, and the two would later work together.

By the mid-eighties, Jean-Michel had become a successful artist, showing and selling work at galleries in New York, Los Angeles and throughout Europe. His work was colourful and messy and his preferred

reference points were the human anatomy, his racial heritage and the work of Leonardo da Vinci. Jean-Michel was interested in codes, symbols, logos and pictograms, all of which are recurring themes in his work. Jean-Michel himself was an engaging presence, reportedly painting in Armani suits then wearing the paint-covered clothing out to his exhibition openings.

Sadly, this creative genius was also troubled with addiction, and it was his heroin addiction that would eventually kill him in 1988. Following the death of friend and collaborator Andy Warhol in 1987, Jean-Michel is said to have become more reliant on the drug, and more depressed. On August 12, 1988 Jean-Michel was found dead in his studio, having suffered from an overdose.

Followers

Today, Jean-Michel's works of art are highly prized. In 2007, one of his untitled pieces sold at Sotheby's in New York for a record price of $14.6 million, and his work has attracted many famous fans. His work tried to say something about Jean-Michel's world and while some elements within his images may be grotesque, they are still desirable to art lovers everywhere.

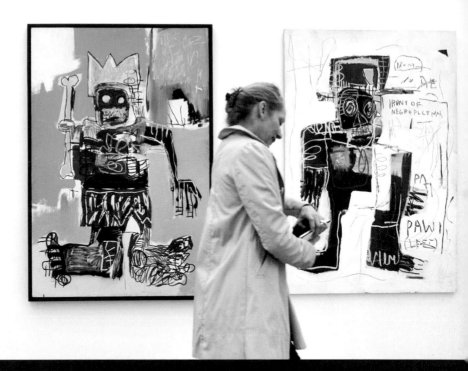

Amy Winehouse

Name: Amy Jade Winehouse

Born: 14 September, 1983

Died: 23 July, 2011

Amy Jade Winehouse was born in North London, to parents Mitch and Janis, the second of two children. Her family was certainly a musical one, and young Amy took a keen interest in jazz music. Her mother had once been engaged to Ronnie Scott (jazz saxophonist and founder of the now legendary Ronnie Scott's Jazz Club in London's Soho). Father Mitch reportedly could often be found singing Frank Sinatra songs to young Amy, and it's obvious that this easy musicality rubbed off on her - Amy was often told off in class for constantly singing and disrupting her classmates.

Early Years

Nine was an important age for Amy's development - as well as the separation of her parents (which by all accounts seems to have been as amicable as it could have been), Amy's grandmother Cynthia suggested that she start going to a theatre school to develop the talents that were obvious even at such a young age. When she was just 10, Amy started a rap group with one of her school friends, called Sweet n' Sour - Amy said that she was the Sour of the title.

Four years later, Amy went to study full-time at the well-respected Sylvia Young Theatre School, where, along with other pupils, she appeared in an episode of the popular sketch show, The Fast Show. Amy stayed there for a short time before getting more training at the BRIT school, alma mater to many other successful British performers, people like Adele and Jessie J. The combination of excellent training at some of Britain's best schools for the performing arts and a huge natural talent meant it was clear Amy was set to be a great performer.

Having acquired her first guitar at the age of 13, and starting to write songs the following year, it was no surprise when a demo tape was sent off by her then-boyfriend, soul singer Tyler James, and she eventually was signed in 2002, to Simon Fuller's 19 Management company. At the start of the contract, and while she was being 'developed' by 19 Amy was kept a secret from other people in the record business. This created more hype round Amy, and when record executives found out about her (by mistake), they started squabbling over this natural talent - a refreshing change from the manufactured pop acts and talent show winners of the day.

Sense Of Style

During Amy's development period, her trademark look was established. As a great fan of girl groups from the 1960s, like The Ronettes, and in particular frontwoman Ronnie Spector, she drew inspiration from their style - in fact this homage to Ronnie Spector was so good that Ronnie once saw a picture of Amy and thought it was herself! The beehive hairdo and heavy eye make-up was to become a look that Amy owned entirely, and often the state of these reflected the state of mind she was in.

Career Beginnings

Amy's debut album, *Frank* was released in October 2003, with the majority of songs on it co-written by

Amy herself. It received wide critical acclaim and huge public support, and in 2004 it was nominated for the prestigious Mercury Music prize. The same year, Amy performed at Glastonbury, V festival and the Montreal Jazz festival.

The next few years saw Amy tour to promote singles from *Frank*, and in 2006, her second album, *Back to Black*, was released. It had a different sound to that of *Frank*, influenced more by those 50s and 60s girl groups than jazz. Again, the album was a huge success, bringing Amy fame and fans from all over the world. Singles like *Rehab*, *Tears Dry On their Own* and *I Told You I Was Trouble* became hits in many countries, and Amy was hot property.

But behind all this professional success, Amy was becoming more and more troubled, and the death of her much-loved grandmother in the middle of 2006 was said to be one of the catalysts for her increasingly bad behaviour. Always someone who spoke her mind and prone to getting into trouble on nights out, Amy's heavy drinking was coupled with drug use, and her often-shambolic private life became fodder for the tabloids.

Warning Signs

When Amy was with (now ex-husband), Blake Fielder-Civil, the subject of many of *Back to Black*'s songs, they were constantly hounded by the paparazzi, who took pictures of them on nights out, often very much the worse for wear. Images showed the couple on nights out, obviously intoxicated and covered in blood and scratches, results of their rows and of injecting heroin.

In 2007, Amy had to cancel some live performances and it was reported that she had suffered an overdose - a potentially lethal combination of heroin, ecstasy, cocaine, ketamine and alcohol.

Amy and Blake split and an extended holiday to St Lucia in early 2009 had early indications that Amy was on the mend. In late 2010, Amy had stated that she had been free of drugs for three years.

A new boyfriend, in film director Reg Traviss, was said to be a stabilising influence in Amy's life. Though their relationship had its ups and downs, the two were reportedly very close and even were engaged, planning to be married in 2012.

Tragic Ending

On July 23 2011, an ambulance was called to Amy's home in Camden, where she was pronounced dead at the scene. She had been found by her security guards in her bed. The post mortem showed no conclusive cause of death, and an inquest was planned for later that year. Some thought her body had gone into shock when she gave up alcohol, while others suspected an overdose. Amy's funeral, on July 26 was attended by many of her friends from the music industry, including Mark Ronson and Kelly Osborne. Fans left tributes outside her Camden home, which quickly became a shrine to one of the most talented female performers of recent times. Amy's legacy will live on way beyond her short years.

The Curse of
27

The Others

Of course, the people listed in the previous pages are in no way an exhaustive list of those that have been struck by The Curse of 27. But just because they're not as famous as some of the other members doesn't make them any less important. Here's a list of some of the other musicians that have died at the age of 27 - you might not have heard of them but why not take this opportunity to find out what you've been missing?

Alexandre Levy, composer, pianist and conductor.
Died January 17, 1892.
Cause of death: Unknown.

Louis Chauvin, ragtime musician.
Died March 26, 1908.
Cause of death: Neurosyphilitic sclerosis.

Nat Jaffe, swing Jazz pianist.
Died August 5, 1945.
Cause of death: Complications from high blood pressure.

Jesse Belvin, R&B singer/songwriter.
Died February 6, 1960.
Cause of death: Car accident.

Rudy Lewis, vocalist of The Drifters.
Died May 20, 1964.
Cause of death: Drug overdose.

Malcolm Hale, lead guitarist of Spanky and Our
Gang.
Died October 30, 1968.
Cause of death: Carbon monoxide poisoning.

Dickie Pride, singer.
Died March 26, 1969.
Cause of death: Overdose of sleeping pills.

Alexandra, singer.
Died July 31, 1969.
Cause of death: Car accident.

Alan Wilson, singer and composer.
Died September 3, 1970.
Cause of death: Barbiturate overdose, possible
suicide.

Arlester "Dyke" Christian, frontman of Dyke &
the Blazers.
Died March 13, 1971.
Cause of death: Murdered.

Linda Jones, soul singer.
Died March 14, 1972.
Cause of death: Complications from diabetes.

Leslie Harvey, guitarist.
Died May 3, 1972.
Cause of death: Electrocution.

Roger Lee Durham, singer and percussionist.
Died July 27, 1973.
Cause of death: Fell off a horse and died from the injuries.

Wallace Yohn, organ player in Chase.
Died August 12, 1974.
Cause of death: Plane crash

Dave Alexander, bassist in The Stooges.
Died February 10, 1975.
Cause of death: Pulmonary edema.

THE CURSE OF 27

ISBN 978 1 907823 22 0